# Chick's Walk



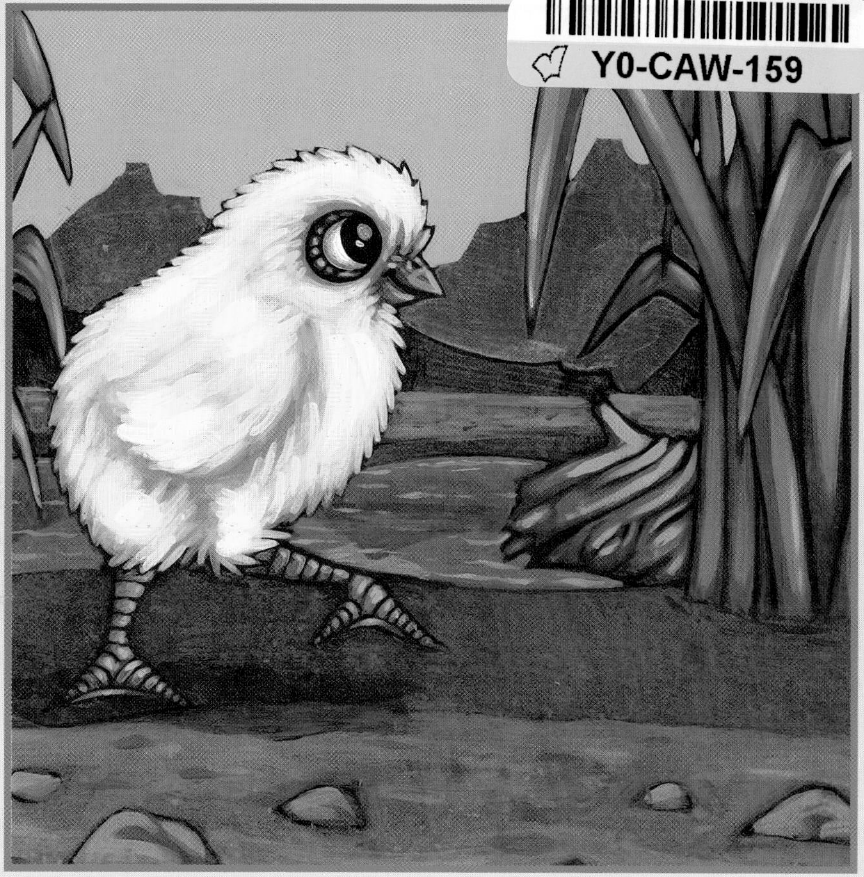

Story by Joy Cowley
Illustrations by Wade Shotter

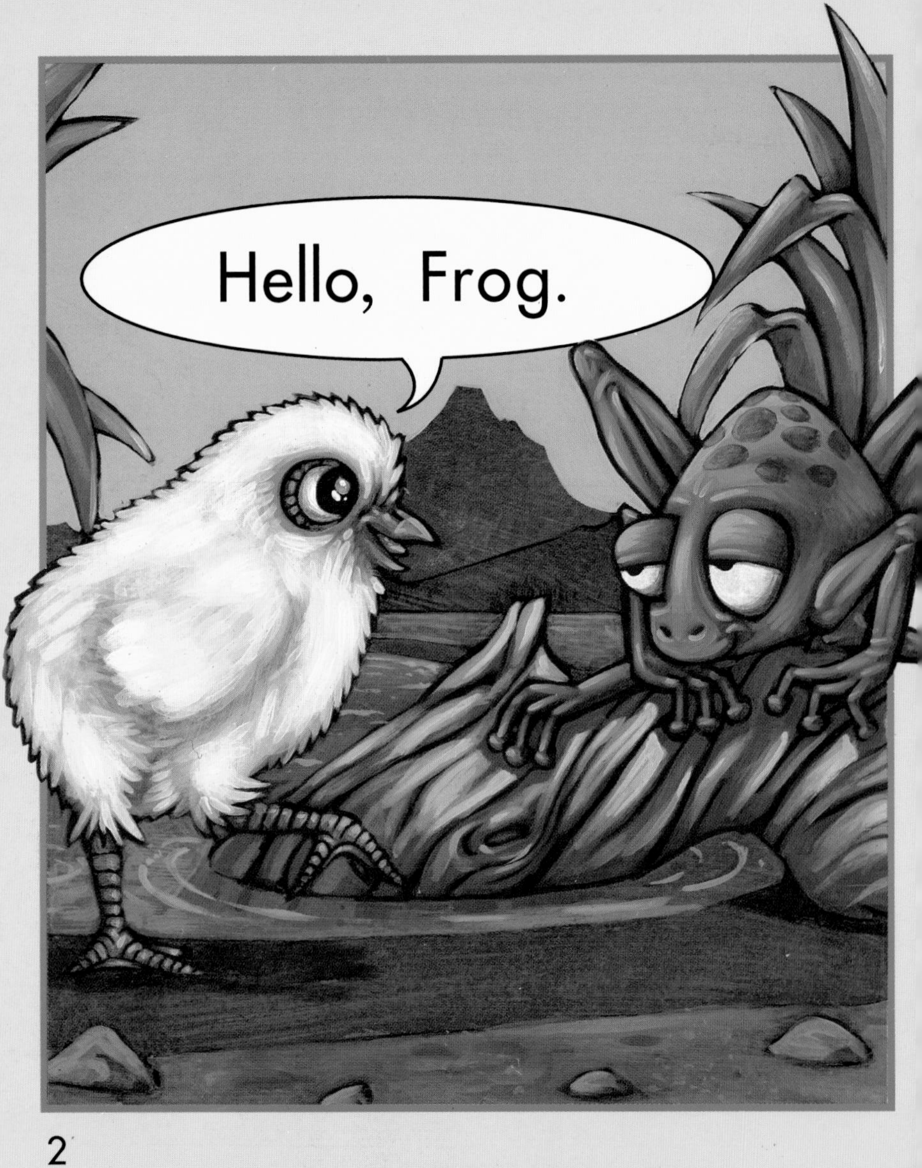
Hello, Frog.

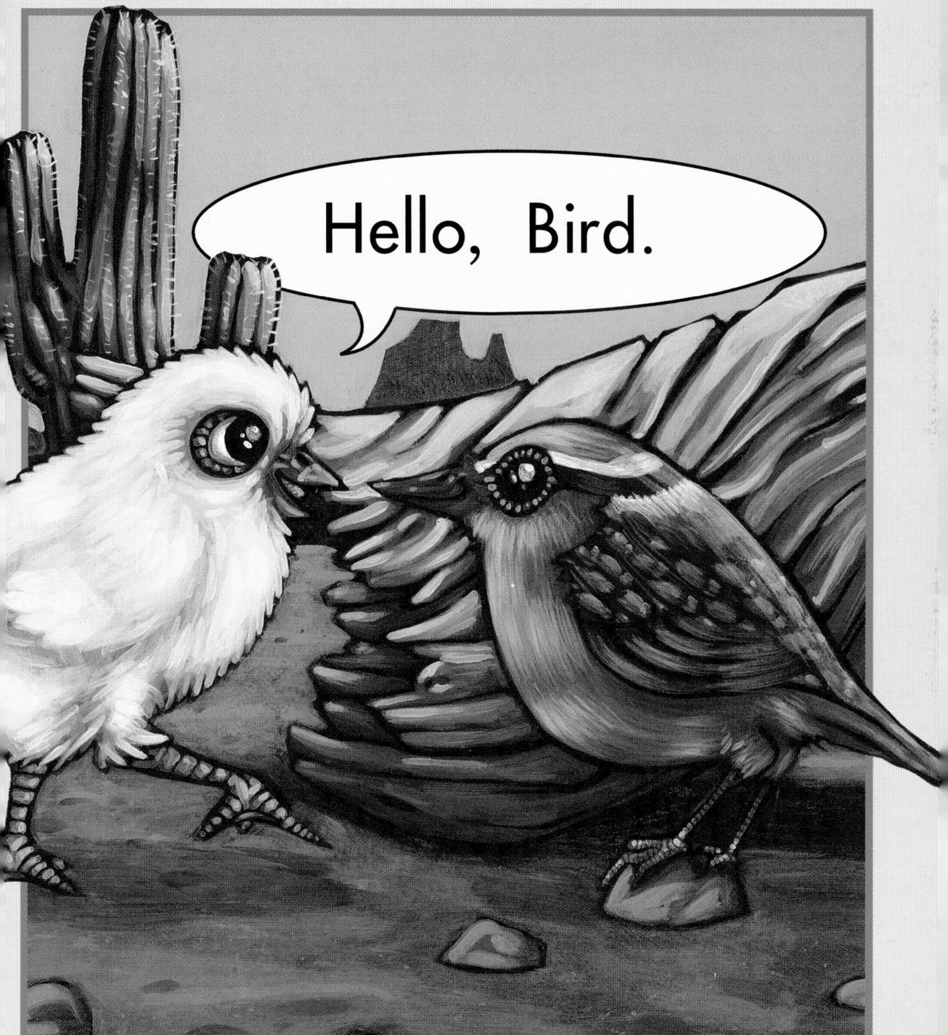
Hello, Bird.

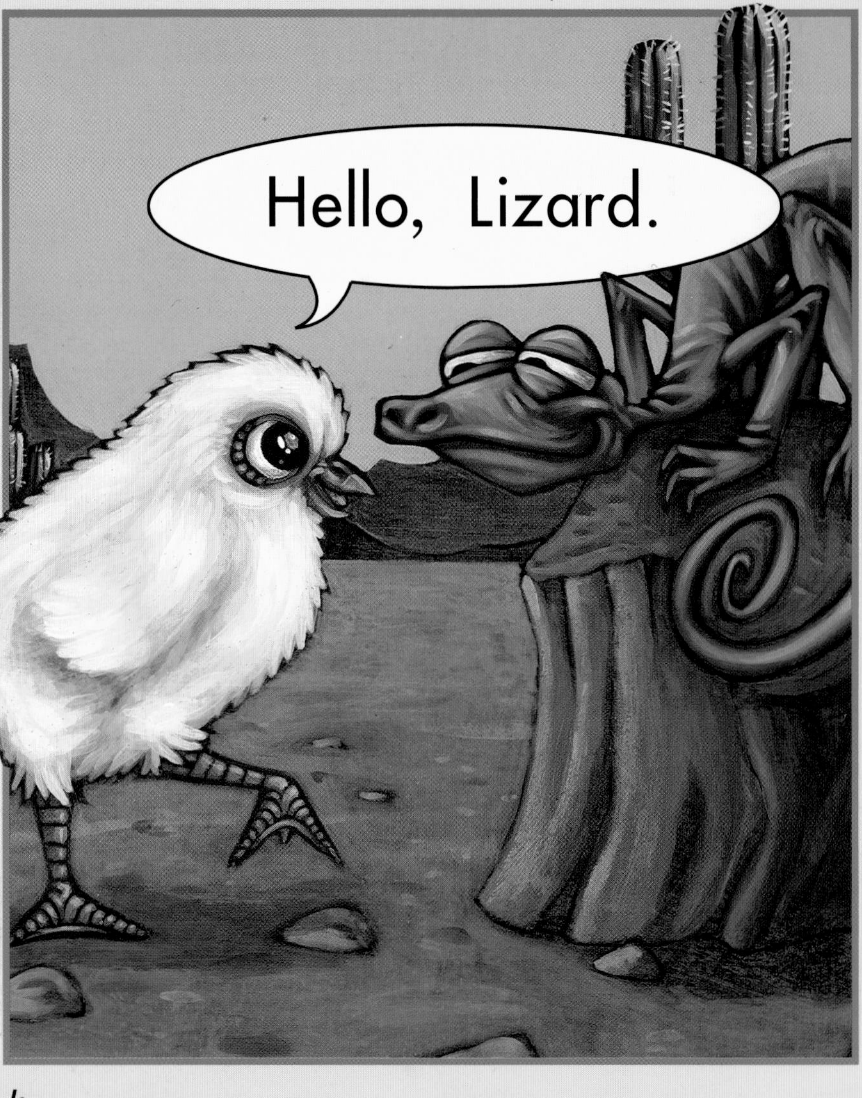
Hello, Lizard.

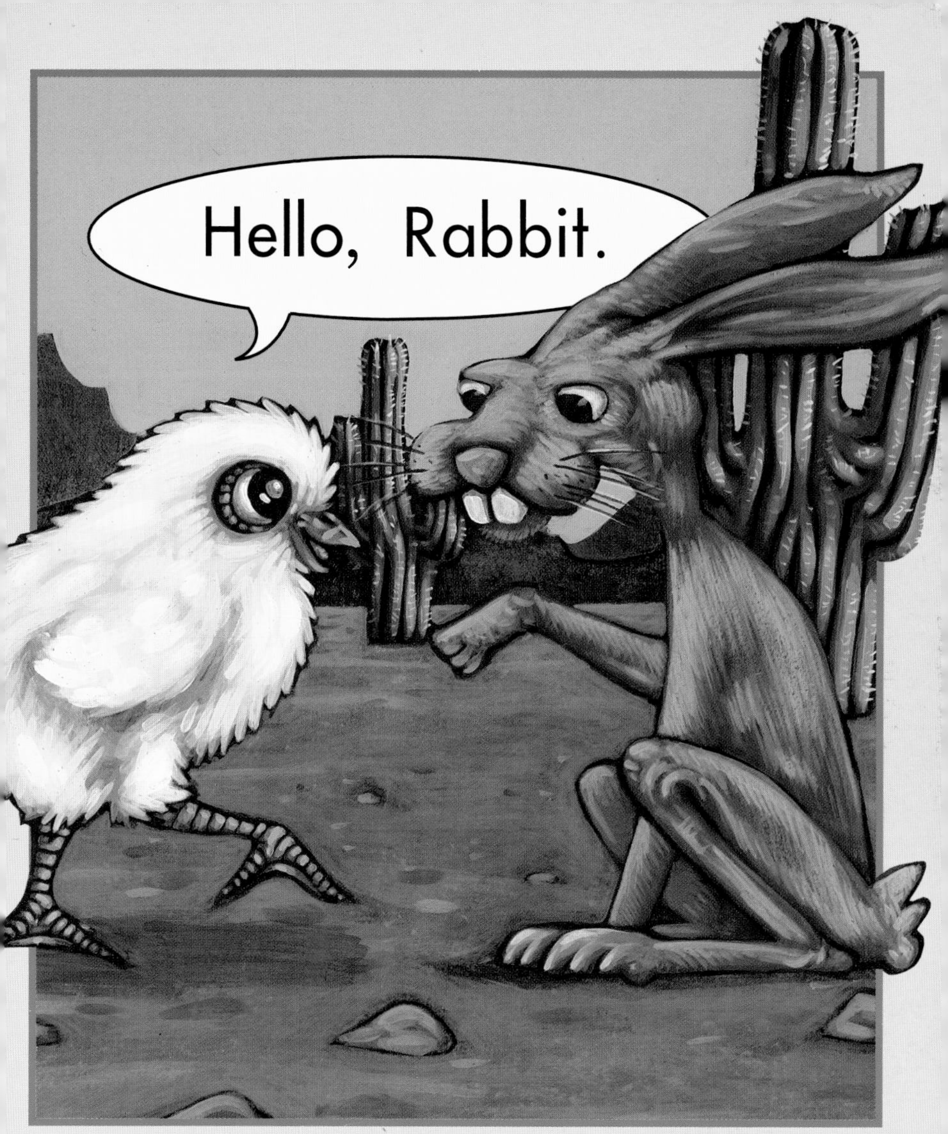
Hello, Rabbit.

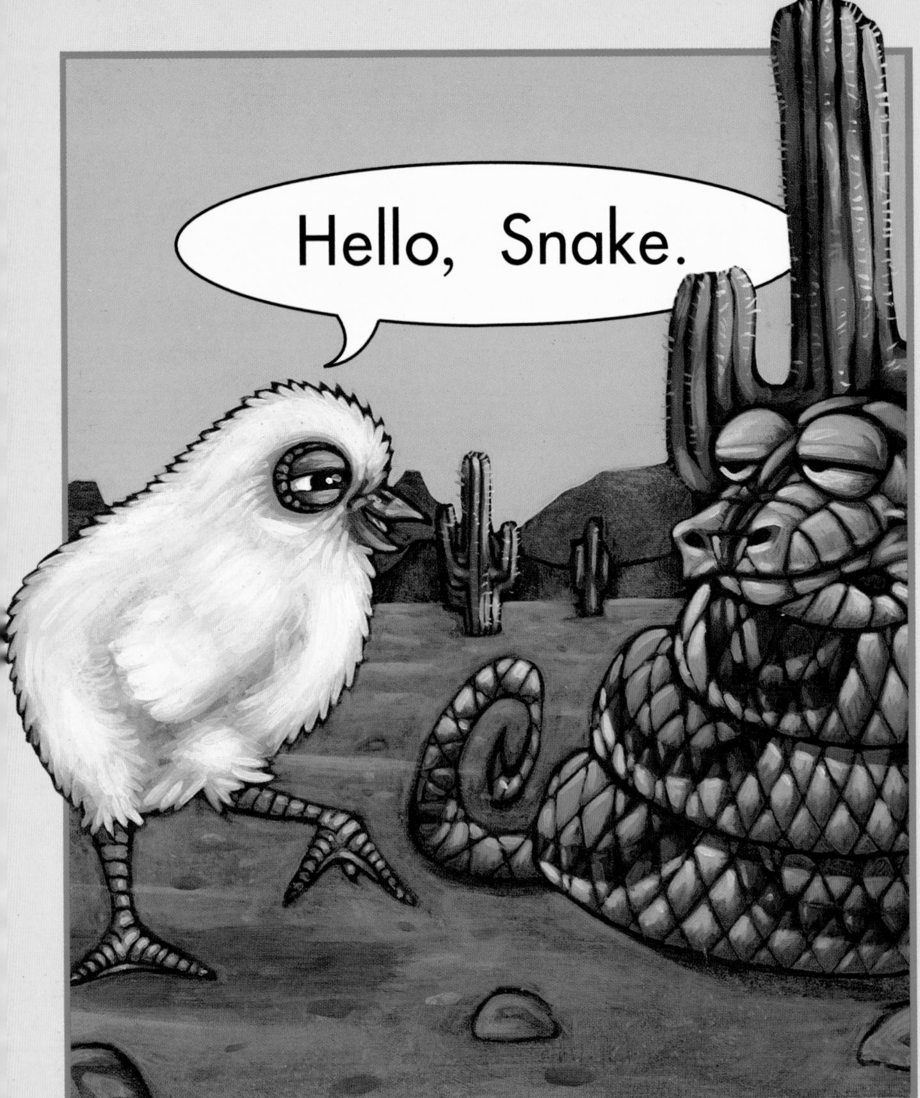
Hello, Snake.

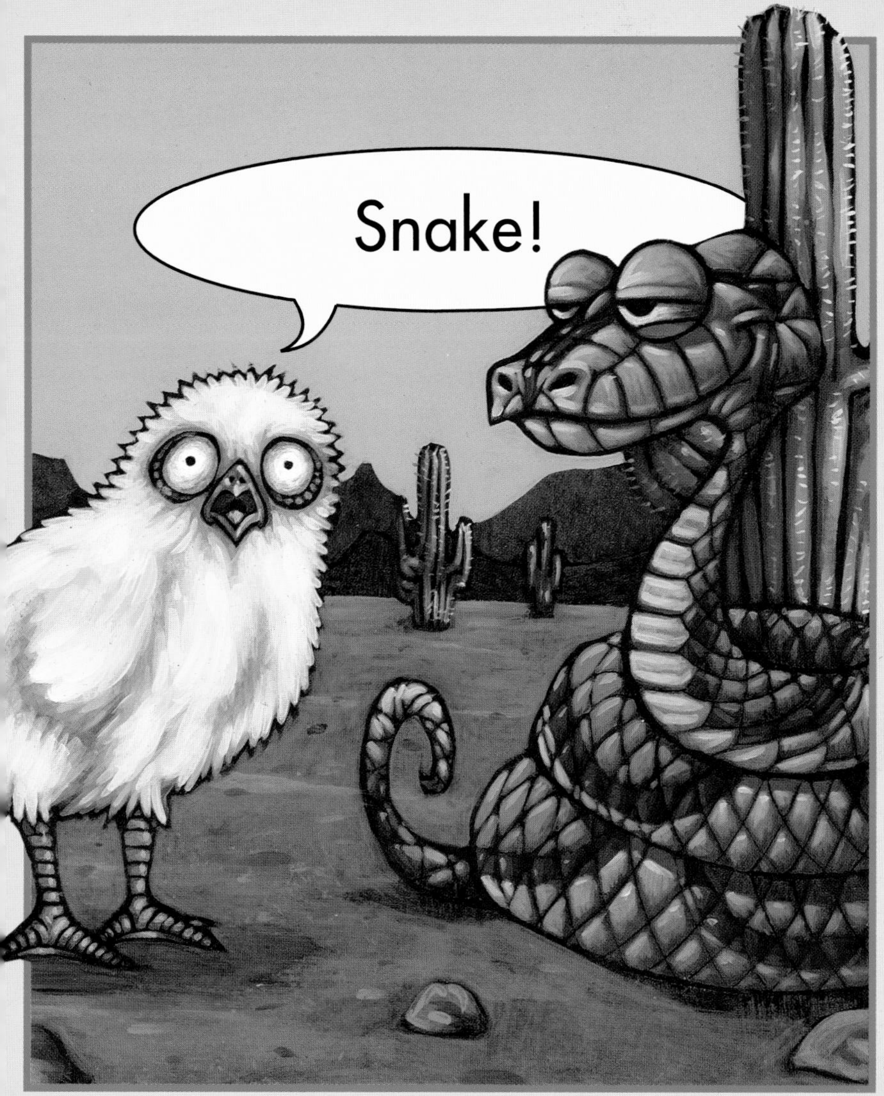
Snake!

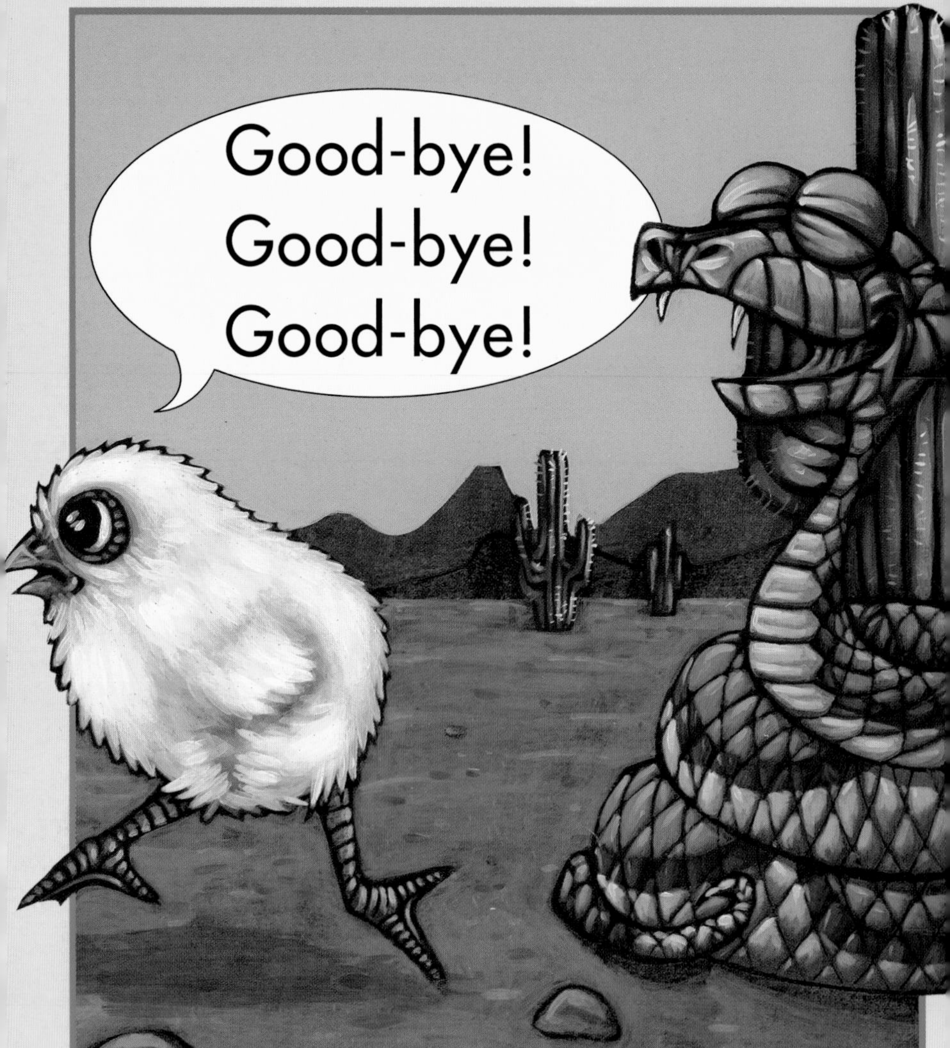
Good-bye!
Good-bye!
Good-bye!